Mark Twain

My Favorite Writer

Wayne Ashmore and Jennifer Nault

WEIGL PUBLISHERS INC.

Published by Weigl Publishers Inc.
350 5th Avenue, Suite 3304, PMB 6G
New York, NY 10118-0069

Website: www.weigl.com
Copyright ©2009 WEIGL PUBLISHERS INC.
All rights reserved. No part of this publication may be reproduced,
stored in a retrieval system, or transmitted in any form or by any means,
electronic, mechanical, photocopying, recording, or otherwise, without
the prior written permission of Weigl Publishers Inc.

Library of Congress Cataloging-in-Publication Data
Ashmore, Wayne.
  Mark Twain : my favorite writer / Wayne Ashmore and Jennifer Nault.
     p. cm.
  Includes index.
  ISBN 978-1-59036-930-2 (alk. paper) -- ISBN 978-1-59036-931-9 (pbk.
: alk. paper)
  1. Twain, Mark, 1835-1910--Juvenile literature. 2. Authors, American--
19th century--Biography--Juvenile literature. 3. Children's stories--
Authorship--Juvenile literature. I. Nault, Jennifer. II. Title.
  PS1331.A88 2008
  818'.409--dc22
  [B]
                                                    2008003972

Printed in the United States of America
1 2 3 4 5 6 7 8 9 0 12 11 10 09 08

Project Coordinator
Heather C. Hudak

Design
Terry Paulhus

Contents

Mark Twain

MILESTONES

1835 Born Samuel Langhorne Clemens on November 25, in Florida, Missouri

1839 Moves to Hannibal, Missouri

1848 Works as a printer's helper

1859 Works as a riverboat pilot on the Mississippi River until the **Civil War** in 1861

1863 Creates his new name, Mark Twain

1865 Publishes his first story, *The Celebrated Jumping Frog of Calaveras County*

1869 Publishes his first best-selling book, *The Innocents Abroad*, after traveling through Europe

1870 Marries Olivia "Livy" Langdon

1876 Publishes the book, *The Adventures of Tom Sawyer*

1885 Publishes his best-known book, *The Adventures of Huckleberry Finn*

1891 Money problems force Mark and his family to leave the United States for Europe

1894 Declares **bankruptcy**

1907 Receives an honorary **doctorate** from Oxford University

1910 Dies in Redding, Connecticut, at age 74

Mark Twain lived during the time of slavery and the Civil War in the United States. Events that took place during this time made him think about **moral** issues and politics. Writing was a way for Mark to express his views on these topics. In many of his books, Mark pointed out what he thought was wrong with society. He often used humor to get across his ideas.

Mark was adventurous, humorous, and thoughtful. Two of his best-known books, *The Adventures of Tom Sawyer* and *The Adventures of Huckleberry Finn*, are adventure stories about young boys. The stories are based on Mark's own life, which was filled with adventure.

Mark Twain published more than two dozen books during his career. He also wrote hundreds of short stories and articles. However, Mark did more than write. He was a great storyteller, and he toured the world giving lectures.

Mark lived until 1910. His books are classics, meaning they have remained popular over time. People around the world continue to read and enjoy his books.

Early Childhood

Samuel Langhorne Clemens was born on November 30, 1835. He started using the name Mark Twain when he became a writer. The first few years of Mark's life were spent in the small town of Florida, Missouri. He was the sixth of seven children. Mark's father was a lawyer and a judge, but he worked at many jobs. The Clemens family was poor and struggled to earn money. To survive, the family often moved from place to place.

In hope of a better life, the Clemens family moved to Hannibal, Missouri, when Mark was four years old. Located on the banks of the Mississippi River, steamboats stopped in Hannibal as they traveled between St. Louis and New Orleans. The town and river activity fascinated Mark. He dreamed of working as a riverboat pilot.

Mark was an unhealthy child. He often was not allowed to play outside because of his poor health. He spent his days dreaming of playing outdoors. However, Mark spent many summers at his uncle John's farm. Uncle John was a very cheerful man. He told fantastic stories and could mimic, or imitate, the voices and behaviors of other people. John liked to play jokes on the children. Young Mark looked up to John and respected his storytelling abilities.

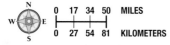

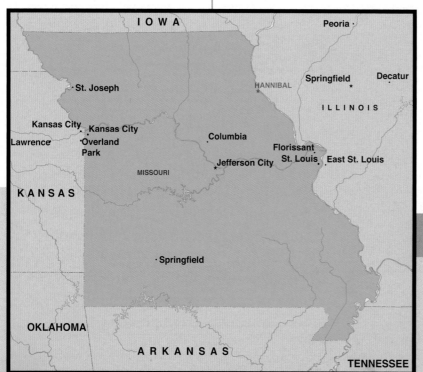

In honor of Mark Twain, Hannibal, Missouri, is home to the Mark Twain Boyhood Home and Museum, The Mark Twain Riverboat, and the Mark Twain Cave Complex.

Mark's favorite place was the farm, and his parents believed farm life improved Mark's health. At the farm, Mark learned about farm chores and animals. He played outdoors and by the river. Mark was not allowed to swim in the river, but he did anyway. He came close to drowning a few times.

When Mark was a child, Missouri was a slave state. In slave states, some people bought and sold other people to work as servants. Many people were taken from their homes in Africa to work as slaves. Mark's uncle owned slaves who worked on the farm. Mark would spend time playing with the slaves in their living quarters. He enjoyed listening to their stories. Some slaves told ghost stories that stayed forever in Mark's memory. One man, nicknamed "Uncle Dan'l," told stories in a fascinating way. Mark wanted to tell stories like Uncle Dan'l.

Mark's father had a slave named Jennie. Jennie took care of Mark and played with him. Once, Mark saw his father punish Jennie. This seemed unfair to Mark. Another time, Mark saw a slave killed by his owner. He began to form opinions about slavery that he would later express in his writing.

Slavery was common in the United States from the early 1600s until 1865.

Growing Up

"Do not put off till tomorrow what can be put off till day-after-tomorrow just as well."
Mark Twain

Mark lived during a time of change and growth in America. Mark had many happy, exciting times. However, laws were not always obeyed, and he **witnessed** violent and disturbing events. Mark saw gunfights and other tragedies. Later, Mark would bring his memories from his childhood to life in his books.

Young Mark liked to have fun and share funny tales. He told stories to get attention and respect from other children. Mark learned that, by telling stories, people would listen to him. By watching other storytellers, and through practice, Mark developed his own storytelling skills. He said funny and strange things. Often, Mark's friends repeated his tales.

A life-size statue of two of Mark's best-known characters, Tom Sawyer and Huckleberry Finn, is located in Hannibal.

Mark attended many schools. For a short time, he went to a private school in Hannibal. Mark also attended a country school. He preferred the country school because it was not as strict as the other schools he had attended. Mostly, Mark felt that school was dull. He had a difficult time sitting still. He longed for freedom and the outdoors. Sometimes, Mark and his friends would stay home from school. They would wander around in search of adventure.

One subject kept Mark interested in school. Spelling was Mark's best subject, and he often won the class spelling bees. Mark always wore the school spelling medal with pride. From a young age, Mark loved to read. He especially enjoyed reading stories about robbers and adventurers.

Inspired to Write

When Mark was a young boy, he made many interesting friends. Later, some of his friends were the inspiration for characters in his novels. One of his best-known characters, Huckleberry Finn, was based on Mark's friend Tom Blankenship. Tom had a difficult childhood. His father was often absent and uncaring. Like Huck, Tom was adventurous and independent.

As a child, Mark liked to read tales about pirates.

When Mark was 12 years old, his father died of **pneumonia**. This forced Mark to take on adult responsibilities. It was a difficult time for his entire family. Though he was barely a teenager, Mark stopped going to school and began working. He first worked as an errand boy. He did odd jobs for the publisher of *The Missouri Courier*. Working for the *Courier* gave Mark a good start in the newspaper business. Next, Mark became a printer's **apprentice** for *The Hannibal Courier*. He arranged the type, or letters, for the stories. In those days, this was a difficult job. The type had to be set by hand, letter by letter. Mark was very quick at setting type, and he would read news from around the world while doing his job.

MARK TWAIN BEGINS HIS LIFE CAREER

IT WAS IN THE SECOND STORY OF THIS BUILDING THAT MARK TWAIN FIRST BEGAN HIS LIFE WORK. HERE HE SET TYPE AND FIRST WROTE FOR THE NEWSPAPER. IT WAS UNDER ONE OF THE WINDOWS THAT HE FOUND THE ARTICLE ON JOAN OF ARC, WHICH CAUSED HIM TO WRITE HER LIFE.
1934

People can take a walking tour through the streets of Hannibal, Missouri, to see places where Mark lived, worked, and played.

10

After two years, Mark joined his brother Orion's newspaper, *The Hannibal Journal*. He worked as a printer and an editorial assistant. This is where Mark developed an interest in writing. He began writing stories, and one **article** was published in the newspaper. Readers liked what they read. They wrote to the paper saying they admired Mark's article. This gave him confidence to keep writing. Mark decided to send another article to other newspapers, and it was published.

After *The Hannibal Journal* was sold, Mark moved many times. He continued to work as a printer, and his skills were highly valued. Mark worked and lived in St. Louis, New York, and Philadelphia. As he took different jobs, he continued to write. By the time he was 25 years old, reading and writing were a part of Mark's daily life.

From May 1870 to April 1871, Mark wrote a column for *The Galaxy*, a monthly magazine.

Favorite Books

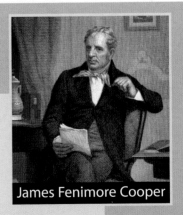

James Fenimore Cooper

Mark enjoyed spending time outdoors, but he also liked reading. Mark's favorite books were adventure novels. When he was young, one of his favorite authors was James Fenimore Cooper. Cooper was a well-known adventure novelist. His best-known novel is *The Last of the Mohicans*. The main character in the book is Hawkeye, who has many forest adventures. Robert Browning was another of Mark's favorite writers. He liked to read Browning's poetry aloud. Mark also read the poetry of Samuel Taylor Coleridge. He was especially fond of the poem *The Rime of the Ancient Mariner*. This is an eerie tale about a ship lost at sea.

Learning the Craft

Mark Twain taught himself to write through practice. He wrote about his own life experiences. It took some time before Mark was able to work as a full-time writer. He tried his hand at many different jobs. Mark lived out his dream of being a riverboat pilot. He panned for gold as a prospector. When this **venture** failed, he went back to writing.

When Mark was 26 years of age, he took a job as a reporter in Virginia City, Nevada. He went to work for his friend Joe Goodman. Joe taught Mark a great deal about newspaper writing. From Joe, Mark learned an important rule of **journalism**. This was to always write the facts. However, Mark found it difficult to tell only the facts. He enjoyed stretching the truth. Before long, Mark got into some trouble at the newspaper. He had written a humorous story about a skeleton that was not true. Although it created quite a stir, more people began to read Mark's writing. He became known for his humorous and clever writing.

A model of the riverboat Mark piloted in his youth is on display at the Mark Twain Museum in Hannibal.

Mark had always been a good storyteller. Writing stories down on paper was the next step. In 1863, he decided to use the name Mark Twain. This name was an old riverboat term, meaning, "two **fathoms** under the **keel**." Riverboats could travel safely in 12 feet (3.7 meters) of water.

Mark moved again. This time, he moved west to San Francisco. There, he took another job as a reporter. Mark did not earn much money, but he got his first big break as an author. A publication in New York called *Saturday Press* printed his story, "Jim Smiley and his Jumping Frog." The story became popular. Before long, it was published across America. This story brought more attention to Mark's work, and he decided to give a **lecture** tour across California. The tour was a success. Mark made extra money and became even more well known.

Joan of Arc believed she had been chosen by God to lead the French into battle against England.

Getting Published

> *"When in doubt, tell the truth."*
> **Mark Twain**

While Mark worked at different jobs across the county, he continued to write. In fact, he wrote many stories that were never finished or published. Still, he kept working at getting his books in print. Mark had a book of short stories published in 1867, called *The Celebrated Jumping Frog and Other Sketches*. Soon after, his writing career soared.

Mark moved to New York and worked for *The Alta California* newspaper. The editors at the newspaper paid for Mark to take a voyage across the Atlantic Ocean. They asked him to write letters describing the voyage. On the ship, Mark met many interesting people. Some of them appear as characters in his first successful novel, *The Innocents Abroad*. The book sold more than 70,000 copies. Mark became quite wealthy.

Mark's voyage was special for another reason. During his trip, Mark saw a picture of a woman named Olivia Langdon. Olivia's brother was onboard the ship, and he arranged for Mark and Olivia to meet. They were engaged a year later.

The Publishing Process

Publishing companies receive hundreds of **manuscripts** from authors each year. Only a few manuscripts become books. Publishers must be sure that a manuscript will sell many copies. As a result, publishers reject most of the manuscripts they receive.

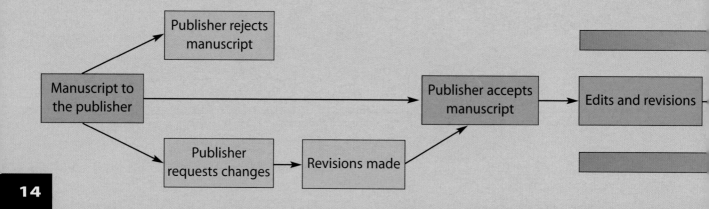

Publisher rejects manuscript

Manuscript to the publisher

Publisher accepts manuscript

Edits and revisions

Publisher requests changes → Revisions made

People bought *The Innocents Abroad* through subscription, or they ordered the book before it was printed. This way, the publishing company knew how many books to print. Mark thought this was a great idea, but he believed he could make more money by publishing his own books. Mark and a partner formed a publishing firm, Charles L. Webster and Company. This company published many books, including Mark's *The Adventures of Huckleberry Finn*.

In addition to Mark's books, his company published the work of other writers. However, Mark lost money in other businesses. He had to declare bankruptcy in 1894, and he lost his publishing company. To pay his debts, Mark went on more lecture tours.

As he grew older, Mark wrote less. Some of the books he wrote got poor reviews. He relied more on his lecturing tours for income. To keep lecturing, Mark and his family moved to Europe. He was well respected in places such as England.

Inspired to Write

Mark Twain was inspired by Helen Keller, a woman who was both hearing and visually impaired, and her caregiver, Anne Sullivan. Anne helped Helen overcome her physical challenges. About Helen, Mark said, "I am filled with the wonder of her knowledge...." He called Anne a "miracle worker." These words were later used as the title of a play about Helen Keller's life, called *The Miracle Worker*.

Once a manuscript has been accepted, it goes through many stages before it is published. Often, authors change their work to follow an editor's suggestions. Once the book is published, some authors receive royalties. This is money based on book sales.

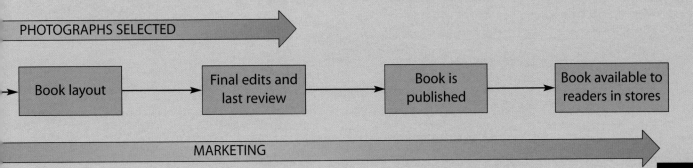

PHOTOGRAPHS SELECTED

Book layout → Final edits and last review → Book is published → Book available to readers in stores

MARKETING

Writer Today

ark Twain died on April 21, 1910, at age 75. Before his death, Mark received honorary degrees from several universities, including Yale and Oxford. Today, people are still interested in his work and in honoring his memory.

Since 1972, the Missouri Association of School Librarians has offered The Mark Twain Award. Missouri children in grades 4 to 8 vote for their favorite book. An award is given to the author of the winning book.

Each year since 2000, The John F. Kennedy Center for the Performing Arts has offered The Mark Twain Comedy Playwriting Award. The $2,500 award is given for the best student-written play.

Founded in the 1100s, Oxford is the oldest university in Great Britain.

Many of Mark's books, such as *The Adventures of Huckleberry Finn*, are still read in schools. However, some schools tried to ban students from reading the *The Adventures of Huckleberry Finn*. In fact, in 2002, this book was ranked by the American Library Association as one of the most banned books in the United States. In the story, Huckleberry tries to protect his friend from a life of slavery. Some people wanted to keep their children from reading about slavery. Mark used the book to raise questions about slavery. He wanted to put an end to slavery, and he used his writing to express these views.

Mark wrote about the poor treatment of African Americans by other Americans. During his travels, he defended human rights in other parts of the world. Mark learned that readers would listen to him if he wrote with humor. Although he used humor, he wished to be taken seriously about the issues he raised.

By reading about Mark Twain's life and his writing, people can learn a great deal about the past. Mark wrote about events in history that are still important. For this reason, courses on Mark's life and writing are taught in colleges and universities today.

Child actor Eddie Hodges played the role of the title character in a movie version of *The Adventures of Huckleberry Finn*.

Popular Books

M ark Twain wrote 28 books in his lifetime. Here are some of his most popular tales.

The Innocents Abroad

The Innocents Abroad was published in 1869. It was Mark's first successful novel. The story is told from the point of view of the narrator. Readers learn about the narrator's adventures on a long trip aboard a steamship called *Quaker City*. The ship sails to many different ports in Europe. It stops in cities such as Paris, Venice, Rome, and Athens. The travelers onboard the ship continue their journey to the Middle East and Egypt. The narrator describes the different places he discovers and the interesting people he meets on the ship. Readers can imagine they are traveling onboard the steamship. *The Innocents Abroad* was based on the letters Mark wrote for *The Alta California* while on a voyage around Europe.

PENGUIN CLASSICS

MARK TWAIN

THE INNOCENTS ABROAD

The Adventures of Tom Sawyer

The Adventures of Tom Sawyer was published in 1876. It is a story about a teenager named Tom Sawyer. He lives by his own rules and is very independent. Tom lives with his Aunt Polly in the small town of St. Petersburg, Missouri, near the Mississippi River. Tom gets in all kinds of mischief. For example, he plays a prank on his Aunt Polly. His punishment is to paint her fence. Tom tricks his friends into painting the fence. Next, Tom meets up with his friend Huckleberry Finn. Tom and Huck witness a crime. They are afraid of the culprit and decide not to tell anyone what they saw. A short time later, the boys go on a treasure hunt. Tom, Huck, and their friend Joe hide out on Jackson's Island. Finally, Tom returns to town, but he and the other boys have been gone for a very long time. The townsfolk think the boys are dead, and they hold a funeral for them. The boys show up at their own funeral. In the end, Tom tells the truth about the crime.

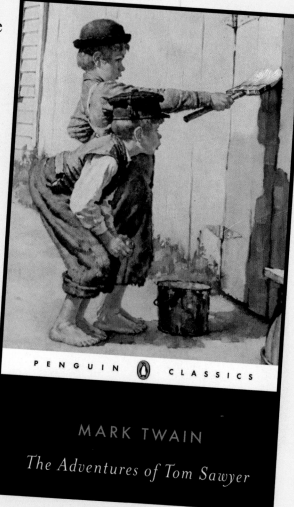

PENGUIN CLASSICS

MARK TWAIN

The Adventures of Tom Sawyer

The Prince and the Pauper

The Prince and the Pauper was published in 1881. It tells the tale of Edward Tudor and Tom Canty. They are two young boys who live in England in the 1500s. Edward is a prince and will one day be the king of England. Tom is a pauper. His family has less money than they need to survive. Edward and Tom look very much alike. One day, Tom and Edward meet at Edward's castle. They notice how much they look alike. For fun, they decide to switch clothing. When Edward is mistaken for Tom, he is thrown out of the castle. Edward has to live life as Tom, and Tom must live as Edward. Edward learns what it is like to be poor, and Tom finds out how the wealthy live.

Eventually, Edward returns to the castle. He proves that he is the real prince, and he becomes the new king. However, Edward now understands how difficult it is to be poor. He tries to make life better for all people in his kingdom. Edward and Tom remain friends.

The Adventures of Huckleberry Finn

The Adventures of Huckleberry Finn was published in 1884. It is a **sequel** to *The Adventures of Tom Sawyer*. Readers first meet Huckleberry as a character in *Tom Sawyer*. In this book, they follow Huck's adventures along the Mississippi River. Readers learn that Huck has run away from his father, who is unkind. Huck fakes his own death. He teams up with an escaped slave named Jim. Together, they go on a rafting adventure down the Mississippi River. Huck and Jim meet up with two crooks. The crooks join Huck and Jim on their trip. The group causes trouble everywhere they go. After the group separates, Huck and Jim meet up with their old friend, Tom Sawyer. The trio causes problems. Tom's Aunt Polly helps get them out of trouble, and she later adopts Huck. Jim learns that the man who kept him as a slave has died. After the man's will has been read, Jim finds out he is free.

PENGUIN CLASSICS

MARK TWAIN

The Adventures of Huckleberry Finn

Creative Writing Tips

Mark Twain wrote almost every day. Still, writing was not always easy for him. Sometimes, he had a difficult time finishing his stories. Other times, Mark would begin a story with excitement, but he would become bored. Mark found it difficult to concentrate. He had trouble keeping an idea in his head long enough to finish a story. It could take months or years before Mark completed certain stories. Still, he kept working on his writing. Over his lifetime, he would publish many works.

Practice Storytelling Aloud

Writing a story is much like telling a story. You can practice telling stories aloud to your friends or classmates. Young Mark developed this ability through practice. He looked up to people who could tell stories well. This included storytellers such as his Uncle John and Uncle Dan'l. Mark Twain once wrote, "The humorous story may be spun out to great length, and may wander around…and arrive nowhere in particular."

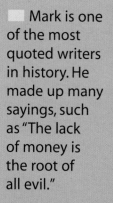

Mark is one of the most quoted writers in history. He made up many sayings, such as "The lack of money is the root of all evil."

Keep a Notebook

Often, Mark would jot a few words in his notebook to record an experience. If dates or fine details were important, Mark might fill a page with notes. Often, he drew sketches of a building or a scene. Later, the sketch would jog his memory. Try keeping a notebook to record your ideas. Observe what you see. Write down funny thoughts or details about a character. Later, you can use these ideas when you begin writing.

Surprise Your Reader

You can plant clues and interesting hints within your story to surprise your readers. Mark said that writing humorous stories took careful planning. The ending was very important. He thought it best to finish with a surprise—something that the readers would not expect. This way, readers learn to stay alert. They pay attention to hints and details in your story.

Read a Variety of Books

Writers learn about writing from the books they read, and Mark Twain read often. It is a good idea to read a wide variety of books. In addition to adventure tales, Mark read poetry, which improved his sense of imagination. Reading different books will help you choose the kinds of stories you want to tell. Take time to visit the school library or a bookstore. Search on the Internet, or ask teachers and librarians for suggestions.

Inspired to Write

Mark Twain's friendships with other writers inspired his work. Harriet Beecher Stowe wrote a book about slavery called *Uncle Tom's Cabin*. Harriet was a close friend and neighbor of Mark's. Harriet and Mark shared their book ideas with each other. They found that they could improve their own ideas by talking about them. Mark wrote his best-known books while living near Harriet.

Mark once said, "The time to begin writing an article is when you have finished it to your satisfaction."

Writing a Biography Review

A biography is an account of an individual's life that is written by another person. Some people's lives are very interesting. In school, you may be asked to write a biography review. The first thing to do when writing a biography review is to decide whom you would like to learn about. Your school library or community library will have a large selection of biographies from which to choose.

Are you interested in an author, a sports figure, an inventor, a movie star, or a president? Finding the right book is your first task. Whether you choose to write your review on a biography of Mark Twain or another person, the task will be similar.

Begin your review by writing the title of the book, the author, and the person featured in the book. Then, start writing about the main events in the person's life. Include such things as where the person grew up and what his or her childhood was like. You will want to add details about the person's adult life, such as whether he or she married or had children.

Next, write about what you think makes this person special. What kinds of experiences influenced this individual? For instance, did he or she grow up in unusual circumstances? Was the person determined to accomplish a goal? Include any details that surprised you.

A concept web is a useful research tool. Use the concept web on the right to begin researching your biography review.

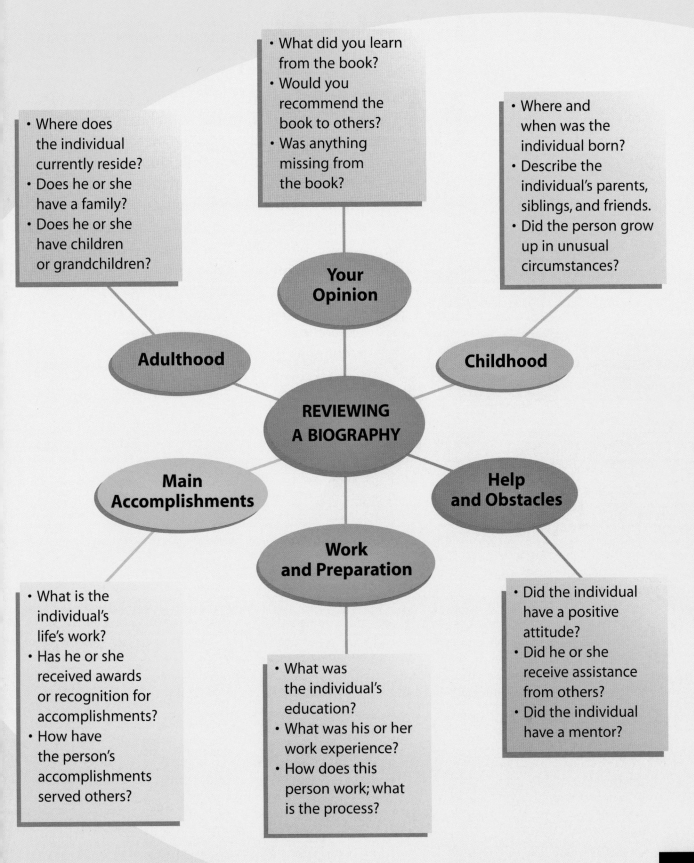

- Where does the individual currently reside?
- Does he or she have a family?
- Does he or she have children or grandchildren?

- What did you learn from the book?
- Would you recommend the book to others?
- Was anything missing from the book?

- Where and when was the individual born?
- Describe the individual's parents, siblings, and friends.
- Did the person grow up in unusual circumstances?

Your Opinion

Adulthood

Childhood

REVIEWING A BIOGRAPHY

Main Accomplishments

Help and Obstacles

Work and Preparation

- What is the individual's life's work?
- Has he or she received awards or recognition for accomplishments?
- How have the person's accomplishments served others?

- What was the individual's education?
- What was his or her work experience?
- How does this person work; what is the process?

- Did the individual have a positive attitude?
- Did he or she receive assistance from others?
- Did the individual have a mentor?

Fan Information

Mark Twain was an excellent lecturer. He spent time lecturing all over the world, sometimes to very large groups. On these trips, he met many people and learned about different cultures. His travels and lectures also gave him a chance to meet his fans. He had some well-known fans, such as author Ernest Hemingway. Hemingway once said, "All modern American literature comes from one book by Mark Twain called *Huckleberry Finn*. All American writing comes from that. There was nothing before. There has been nothing as good since."

In total, Mark wrote 28 books, as well as many letters, sketches, and stories.

At one time, Mark received bags of letters from fans. Children wrote to ask Mark for writing tips. The mail delighted Mark, and he tried to answer the letters when he had time.

Many of Mark's books have been made into movies, including *The Prince and the Pauper* and *The Adventures of Huckleberry Finn*. Mark also wrote plays and made some of his novels into plays. One of his plays, *Is He Dead?*, was recently discovered. The play is a comedy about a painter who fakes his own death to raise the value of his art. It was performed on Broadway in New York City in 2007. Other Mark Twain plays continue to be staged across North America.

An entire museum is devoted to Mark Twain. The Mark Twain Boyhood Home & Museum in Hannibal, Missouri, promotes Mark's life and work. It has a collection of items and papers related to Mark Twain. Visitors can take a guided tour of the museum to learn more about this writer.

WEB LINKS

The Official Website of Mark Twain
www.cmgww.com/ historic/twain
Fans can visit Mark's official website to can read some of his quotes. There is a biography and a list of all of the books and articles Mark wrote.

Mark Twain Boyhood Home & Museum Website
www.marktwainmuseum.org
This site has information about what visitors can expect to see at the museum. There is a listing of events and research tools.

Quiz

Q: About how many books did Mark Twain publish during his career?

1

A: 28

2

Q: Where did Mark live as a child?

A: Hannibal, Missouri

3

Q: What was Mark Twain's birth name?

A: Samuel Langhorne Clemens

Q: Who wrote *Uncle Tom's Cabin*?

A: Harriet Beecher Stowe

Q: What was Mark's best subject in school?

A: Spelling

Q: Where did Mark work as a printer's apprentice?

A: The Hannibal Courier

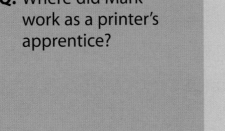

Q: What was special about the two main characters in *The Prince and the Pauper*?

A: They looked similar.

Q: Where was Mark's favorite place to go as a boy?

A: His Uncle John's farm

Q: When Mark was a child, what did he dream of becoming as an adult?

A: A riverboat pilot

Q: What book was the sequel to *The Adventures of Tom Sawyer*?

A: The Adventures of Huckleberry Finn

Writing Terms

This glossary will introduce you to some of the main terms in the field of writing. Understanding these common writing terms will allow you to discuss your ideas about books and writing with others.

action: the moving events of a work of fiction

antagonist: the person in the story who opposes the main character

autobiography: a history of a person's life written by that person

biography: a written account of another person's life

character: a person in a story, poem, or play

climax: the most exciting moment or turning point in a story

episode: a short piece of action, or scene, in a story

fiction: stories about characters and events that are not real

foreshadow: hinting at something that is going to happen later in the book

imagery: a written description of a thing or idea that brings an image to mind

narrator: the speaker of the story who relates the events

nonfiction: writing that deals with real people and events

novel: published writing of considerable length that portrays characters within a story

plot: the order of events in a work of fiction

protagonist: the leading character of a story; often a likable character

resolution: the end of the story, when the conflict is settled

scene: a single episode in a story

setting: the place and time in which a work of fiction occurs

theme: an idea that runs throughout a work of fiction

Glossary

apprentice: a person who is being trained by another person, often to learn a trade

article: a piece of nonfiction writing, usually written for a newspaper or magazine

bankruptcy: to declare under the law that one has no money

Civil War: an armed conflict that took place between the northern and southern states from 1861 to 1865

doctorate: the highest degree awarded by a college or university

fathoms: units of length that are equal to 6 feet (1.8 m)

journalism: the work of reporting, writing, and editing news stories

keel: the structure at the centerline of the bottom of a boat

lecture: an educational speech given in front of an audience

manuscripts: drafts of a story before it is published

moral: having to do with what is right and wrong, good or fair

pauper: a person who is very poor

pneumonia: a disease that affects the lungs

sequel: a book that carries the story over from another book

venture: a risky business opportunity

witnessed: saw something happen

Index

Photo Credits

Every reasonable effort has been made to trace ownership and to obtain permission to reprint copyright material. The publishers would be pleased to have any errors or omissions brought to their attention so that they may be corrected in subsequent printings.

Photo credits:
Weigl acknowledges Getty Images as its primary photo supplier.
Other credits include: Penguin Books: pages 18 to 21.